Cupcake

Coloring Book

Coloring Pages for Kids

All rights reserved. No part of this document may be reproduced Used or transmitted in any form or by any means, electronic or otherwise. This means you cannot photocopy any material ideas or tips that are provided in this book.

Coloring Book for Kids
Published by Ciparum LLC

Cupcake Coloring Book
© 2016 Ciparum LLC
All rights reserved.
ISBN-10:1-944741-40-2
ISBN-13:978-1-944741-40-2

www.coloringpagesforkids.co

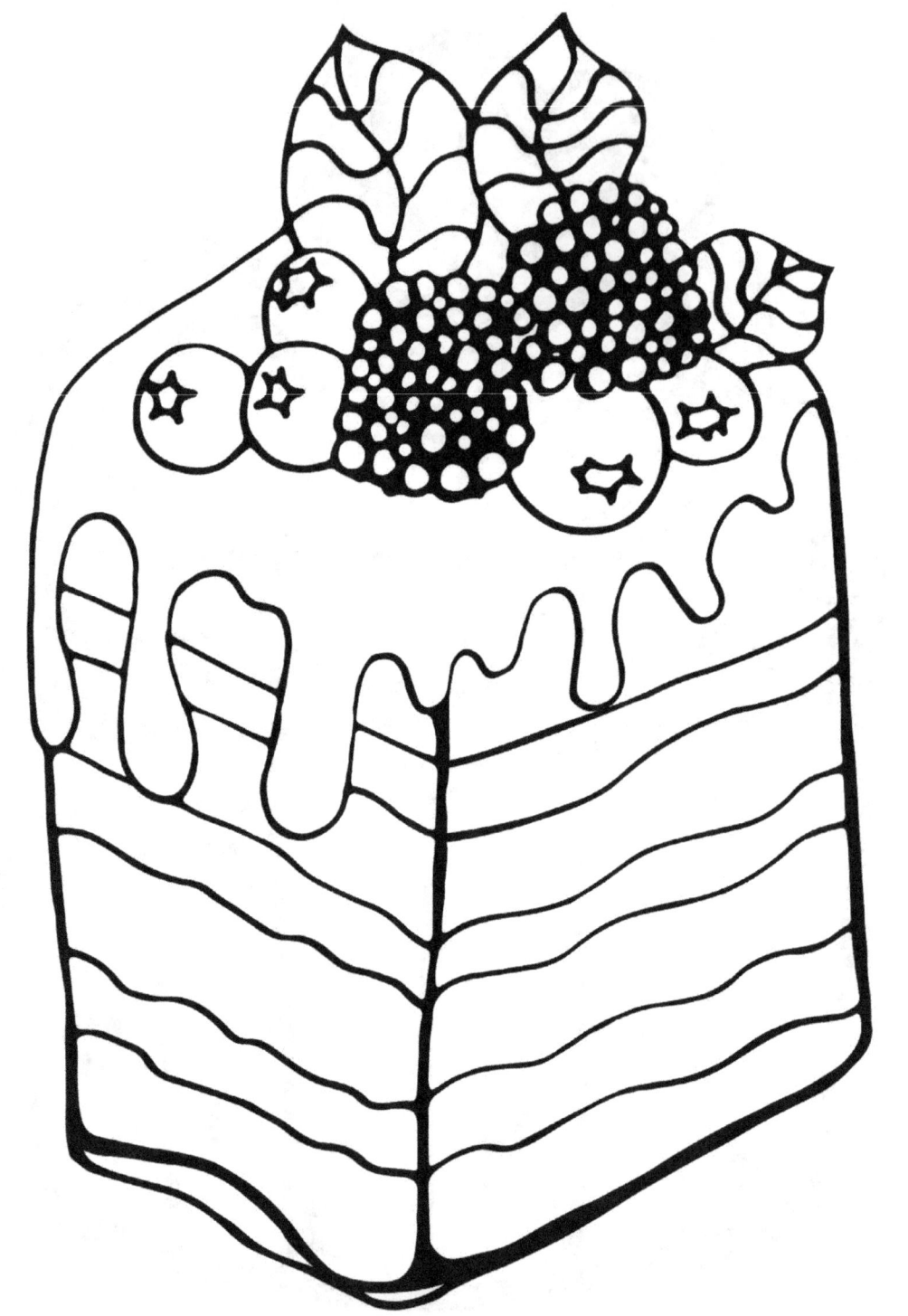

Other Books in this Series

Pirate Coloring Book
Easter Coloring Book
Ghosts and Ghouls Coloring Cook
Pirate Coloring Book
Zombie Coloring Book
Valentine's Day Coloring Book
Saint Patrick's Coloring Book
Halloween Coloring Book
Dracula Coloring Book
…and a lot more!

Others

Handwriting for Preschool and up
Learn How to Draw

For more engaging activity books, visit:

www.ColoringPagesforKids.co

www.ingramcontent.com/pod-product-compliance
Lightning Source LLC
Chambersburg PA
CBHW081358080526
44588CB00016B/2534